

STOMACH!
CHOKE

ANYTHING TO HELP YOU HEAL, MR BROWN

EASY TIGER!!
NO...!

DON'T STOP LYING

SCOOBY-DOO
Thank you Mistress Daphne for saving me from that evil hypnotist
Your welcome my little slave I'm just glad I didn't Get there to soon

SCOOBY COCK, WHERE ARE YOU!
MMMNNN! BIG COCK

OH OH AAHHH!!!
SORRY LOIS
I CAN'T HOLD IT
ANY LONGER.

MARGE
EROTIC FANTASIES
LOVE in the TIME of SCURVY

Daddy's
Lucky You

SEXY 101
MY NAME IS MS. RYLES
APPLE BOTTOM

SCOOBY-DOO!

Marquis

www.ingramcontent.com/pod-product-compliance
Lightning Source LLC
Chambersburg PA
CBHW082347220526
45470CB00008B/2671
9781978078284